Derbyshire Recipes

A selection of traditional Derbyshire recipes

By **Amanda Wragg**

BRADWELL
BOOKS

Published by Bradwell Books

9 Orgreave Close Sheffield S13 9NP

Email: books@bradwellbooks.co.uk

©Amanda Wragg 2013

British Library Cataloguing in Publication Data: a catalogue record for this book is available from the British Library.

1st Edition

ISBN: 9781902674858

Print: Cambrian Printers, Aberystwyth, Ceredigion. SY23 3TN

Design by: Andrew Caffrey

Edited by: Louise Maskill

Photographic Credits:
  Andrew and Susan Caffrey, Joan Ransley & ShutterStock

Front cover:
  Left to right: travellight/Shutterstock; Bakewell Pudding Shop; Jamie Rogers/Shutterstock;
  Magdalena Kucova/Shutterstock
  Bottom: Andrew and Susan Caffrey

Back Cover:
  Bakewell Pudding Shop

Title page:
  Main-Joan Ransley; inset-Magdalena Kucova/Shutterstock

The photographs used in this book are to illustrate the dish and are not meant as a final representation of the finished result. Any garnish or additions are at your discretion.

Contents

Introduction

It's said that the **Peak District** is the second most visited national park in the world after Mount Fuji. It's not hard to believe; from the magnificent Howden, Ladybower and Derwent dams in the north to breathtaking Lathkilldale, Dovedale and Milldale in the south, an incredibly varied and often dramatic landscape unfolds; towering hills, unique limestone crags and wild moorland, sheltered woodland rich in animal and plant life and deep, velvety valleys – all there for the taking.

If you're a foodie you're never going to go hungry – Derbyshire is chock-full of great pubs and restaurants, cafes and delis. I was born and raised in the Peak District, and went to school in Bakewell, home of the internationally famous Bakewell Pudding (different from the tart!)

and my mum, a busy country pub landlady cooked hearty, traditional Derbyshire dishes using fabulous local produce – I was practically weaned on oatcakes, eaten on their own (fried, with a sprinkling of salt) or filled with mushrooms, cheese or tomatoes – a great supper dish, and so easy to make in your own kitchen. 'Lobby' is a rustic stew made with Derbyshire lamb – we had it with either dumplings or – a very niche North Derbyshire quirk – on pancakes.

From Fidgety pie, a simple, wholesome savoury dish which has its beginnings in ancient history to Ashbourne Gingerbread, introduced (so legend has it) by an incarcerated French General during the Napoleonic War, Derbyshire has a wealth of traditional recipes to try at home.

Andrew & Susan Caffrey

Soda Bread

Baking is back! Making your own bread is very satisfying – and easy. This simple, straightforward recipe will become part of your weekly routine – you've got a home baked loaf in under an hour. Buttermilk is easy to buy in supermarkets these days – but if you can't get hold of it, use plain live yoghurt instead. Once you've made one you'll never go back to shop bought. **The smell in the kitchen whilst this is baking will send you off the scale!**

Ingredients

400g wholemeal flour

75g plain white bread flour

1 tsp sea salt

1 tsp bicarbonate of soda

425ml buttermilk or plain live yoghurt

Method

1. Preheat the oven to 390F/200C/gas 6. Put all the dry ingredients into a large bowl and mix together. Make a well in the centre and pour in the buttermilk or yoghurt. Using your hands mix all the ingredients until you've got a soft, slightly sticky dough.

2. Tip it out on to a lightly floured work surface and knead lightly for about a minute, just long enough to pull it together into a loose ball but no longer - you need to get it into the oven while the bicarb is still working.

3. Put the dough on a lightly floured baking sheet and dust generously with flour. Mark a deep cross in it with a sharp knife, cutting about two-thirds of the way through the loaf. Bake for 40-45 minutes, until the loaf sounds hollow when tapped underneath.

4. Cool on a wire rack if you like a crunchy crust, or wrap in a clean tea towel if you prefer a soft crust. Soda bread is best eaten while still warm, spread with salty butter and/or a dollop of your favourite jam or lemon curd. It makes great toast the next day — that's if you've got any left!

Space Monkey Pics/ShutterStock

Vegetable Stock

Since time immemorial country people the world over have kept the stockpot simmering all day on the kitchen stove. Those days are pretty much gone, but making a good basic stock isn't difficult and although there are many quick options these days (even one or two of our 'top' chefs are advertising stock cubes!) there's nothing as satisfying as knowing your soup, stew or casserole is made with the real deal. This flavoursome stock will last for up to a week in the fridge, or batch freeze it for later use. Many cooks make different stocks depending on what they're the basis of; beef, fish, chicken – but I find this basic stock will do nicely for any dish you're making.

Ingredients

3 medium onions

5 medium carrots

3 medium leeks

3 sticks celery

8 cabbage leaves

Handful flat leaf parsley

3 sprigs fresh thyme

1 bay leaf

Sea salt

3.5 litres cold water

Method

1	Roughly chop the vegetables and put in a large saucepan or stockpot with all the other ingredients.
2	Cover with water and bring slowly to the boil.
3	Reduce the heat to a gentle simmer. Skim off any scum.
4	Simmer very gently with the lid ajar for an hour, skimming from time to time.
5	Strain through a sieve – don't push any of the soft vegetables through as the stock will become cloudy. Allow to cool then refrigerate.

Ben Smith/ShutterStock

Simple Tomato Sa

You know that feeling after a hard day's work, and you just want to throw a simple supper together? This delicious, easy tomato-based sauce is great with pasta — all you need add is a grating of parmesan, a sprinkling of basil and a glass of red wine. Sorted.

Ingredients SERVES 2

Olive oil

1 red onion, finely chopped

1 clove of garlic, finely chopped

A handful of black olives, stoned and halved

Pinch of chilli flakes

Tin of chopped tomatoes

1 tsp sugar

Sea salt

Freshly ground black pepper

4 basil leaves

Pasta of your choice — literally any will do; spaghetti, penne, linguine or those cute little bow ties

Method

1   Warm a slug of olive oil in a frying pan. Add the
    chopped onion and garlic and cook gently until
    starting to colour. Add the chilli flakes, sugar, olives
    and the tin of tomatoes. Season to taste.

2   Let it bubble for about 15 minutes (adding a bit of
    water if it's starting to look dry)

3   In the meantime cook your pasta in a large pan of
    boiling salted water. Drain, put in warm bowls and
    drop the tomato sauce on the top. Grate parmesan
    on the top and finish with the basil leaves.

Sergey Andrianov/ShutterStock

Marilyn Barbone/ShutterStock

Pickled Red Cabb

This tasty (and easy to make) accompaniment to cheese and meat is also a great idea for a present if you find a pretty jar to put it in. It takes a bit of time but it's worth it. It works brilliantly well with hotpot — or indeed any kind of stew or casserole. At home we seemed to have a bowl of on the table with every meal.

The cabbage is steeped in salt for about 3 hours then boiled for around 40 minutes.

Ingredients

500g red cabbage

140g sea salt

500ml cider vinegar

200ml red wine

400g granulated sugar

2 tsp black peppercorns

6 bay leaves

2 tbsp yellow mustard seeds

2 red chillies sliced very thin

Method

1. Place the shredded cabbage in a colander over the sink and sprinkle with salt. Leave for 2-3 hours, then drain and wash away the salt. Pay dry with a clean tea towel.

2. Put the vinegar, wine, sugar, peppercorns and bay leaves into a big, wide saucepan and simmer until the liquid has reduced by about half – about 40 minutes.

3. Strain through a fine sieve into a jug or bowl, and discard the peppercorns and bay leaves. Put the cabbage and mustard seeds into a big bowl, and then pour the strained liquid over.

4. Transfer the cabbage and pickling liquid into sterilised jars and seal. It will last up to a month in the fridge.

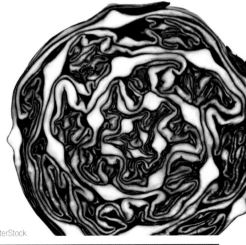

M. Unal Ozmen/ShutterStock

Short Crust Pastry

Ready made pastry is a quick, convenient option if you're short of time, but if you'd rather make your own (it's simple enough) here's a fool-proof recipe that takes minutes to make, and just think of the brownie points you'll earn when the family knows you've made it from scratch!

Ingredients

125g plain flour

Pinch of salt

55g butter, cubed

40ml cold water

Method

1   Put the flour and salt in a large bowl and add the cubes of butter. Use your fingertips to rub the butter into the flour until you have a mixture that resembles coarse breadcrumbs — make sure you've no big lumps of butter left. It's true that cool hands helps!

2   Using a knife, stir in just enough of the cold water to bind the dough together. Wrap the dough in clingfilm and chill for 10 minutes before using. Once chilled, roll out on a lightly floured work top to the required size for your pie or pasty. Job done!

The Best Gravy ir

There are as many recipes for gravy as there are cookery books, but this is the Derbyshire (and therefore the best) way.

Ingredients

Juices from the Sunday roast

1 tbsp plain flour

A splash of balsamic vinegar

2-3 dashes Worcestershire Sauce

Salt and freshly ground black pepper

Method

1   Scrape the bottom of the pan from your roast whilst the meat's resting and gather together all the sticky, brown, gooey bits in one corner of the pan. Mix the flour in and put the tin over two rings of the hob. Slowly, add a couple of tablespoons of boiling water and keep stirring as it thickens – keep adding water until it's lovely and thick.

2   Add the vinegar, relish and seasoning. Add another 300ml hot water and bring to the boil. Let it simmer for about 20 minutes – it will reduce a bit, leaving you with an intense, meaty, dark golden gravy that you can use with any number of dishes.

Christopher Elwell/ShutterStock

Derbyshire Oatcak

These wonderful savoury pancakes have been a Derbyshire delicacy since the 17th century. They're a cross between a crumpet and a pancake – soft, round and pliable. They were traditionally cooked on hot gritstone found in the Ashover area; my mum used to fry them in dripping until they were crisp, then we'd sprinkle salt on them and have them for tea. Doesn't seem to have done us any harm! You'll find them in butcher's shops all over the county, and they're often found on hotel breakfast menus served with a poached egg on top. Delicious.

Ingredients

225g fine oatmeal

1 tsp salt

14g fresh yeast

285ml warm milk and water mixed

½ tsp sugar

Vegetable oil

Method

1 In a large bowl, mix together the flour, oatmeal and salt. Dissolve the yeast with a little of the warm water and add the sugar. Once it becomes frothy, pour it into the dry ingredients, gradually adding the rest of the milk and water, beating well to form a thin batter.

2 Cover with a wet cloth and rest for half an hour until the mixture has risen.

3 Heat a griddle or frying pan and add a small slug of vegetable oil. Scoop a cupful of the batter and pour it carefully into the hot pan. Cook for about 4 minutes on each side, turning when the upper side appears dry and the underside is golden. Ideally you want them roughly the same size as a side plate.

4 They keep well in the fridge for a few days and they freeze well too; top tip: put a layer of cling film between each one so that you can take them out of the freezer one by one.

5 Once they're made, try serving them with different fillings. Thinly sliced mushrooms and a handful of grated cheese works really well; warm some oil in a frying pan and put the oatcake in. Once it's warmed through, put the mushrooms and cheese on half of the cake then turn the other half down – like a pancake. The cheese will melt and the cake will crisp. Kids love these!

Jamie Rogers/ShutterStock

Leek & Potato Sou

A proper winter warmer! This nutritious soup is quick and easy to make, light both in calories and on the pocket. Double the ingredients if you want to put half in the freezer – it keeps really well. A swirl of cream in the bowl is a luxurious finish; serve with thick, crusty bread*

Ingredients

25g butter or **2 tbsp** olive oil

4 leeks, green tops removed and washed in salty water to remove any soil

2 large potatoes, peeled and cut into dice

1 ltr vegetable stock (Marigold or Kallo cube)

¼ pint milk

Sea salt and freshly ground black pepper

Method

1. Gently heat the butter or oil in a large heavy based pan. Add the leeks and potato and soften for 5 minutes. Add the stock and bring to the boil. Season, turn down to a simmer and cook for 20 minutes.

2. Add the milk and cook for a further 5 minutes. Take it off the heat and let it cool a bit before blending (with a stick or in an electric blender – either way, make sure it's super smooth.) If it's too thick, add a splash of milk

Richard Griffin/ShutterStock

Hartington Cheese

Hartington Cheese Company Shop

These tasty tarts are simple to make and easy on the purse. Eat them warm or cold – either way you can't fail to impress the family or dinner guests. Cheese has been made in the stunning village of Hartington for generations; they closed for a while but they're up and running again. It's worth calling in to the shop, the selection is wide. The deliciously soft, mild Dovedale Blue is a particularly good option for this recipe.

Ingredients SERVES 4

Packet ready-made short crust pastry or make you own, P14

1 onion, thinly sliced

1 red pepper, thinly sliced

150g Hartington cheese

120ml double cream

1 medium egg

1 sprig thyme, leaves removed and finely chopped

Sea salt and freshly ground black pepper

Method

1 Pre-heat the oven to 375F/190C/gas
   5. Roll out the pastry to the thickness
   of a pound coin on a lightly floured
   surface. Line the pastry cases then top
   with a disk of greaseproof paper and
   baking beans. Cook for 10 minutes.

2 Remove the paper and beans and
   cook for a further 5 minutes. Remove
   and leave to cool.

To make the filling:

3 Gently fry the onion and red pepper in
   a tablespoon of olive oil until they're
   soft but not brown. Divide between the
   four cases. Crumble the cheese on
   top of the onions.

4 Whisk the cream and egg together,
   add the thyme, season and pour into
   the cases

5 Cook in the middle of the oven for
   15 minutes (the pastry will be a lovely
   golden brown and the cheese mix
   bubbling). Serve hot or cold with a
   green salad and a fat slice of
   brown bread.

Joan Ransley

This healthy salad is very easy salad to assemble and full of summer colour. It's a great starter to a supper party, a side dish if you're having a barbeque, and if you add a handful of your favourite crumbly cheese, a main course. Serve with a chunk of home made bread.

Ingredients SERVES 4

700g assorted tomatoes – vine are the sweetest, but use baby plum too, and as many colours as you can find

Sea salt

Freshly ground black pepper

¼ tsp caster sugar

Handful of basil leaves

6 tbsp olive oil

8 slices prosciutto

Handful of black olives

Prosciutto

Method

1. Halve, slice or quarter the tomatoes depending on their size.

2. Arrange on a large plate and sprinkle with the salt, pepper and sugar.

3. Leave for about half an hour. Tear the basil leaves on the tomatoes, pour over the olive oil and drape the prosciutto over the top. If you're bulking it up a bit, crumble the cheese over, chuck the olives on and serve with a fat slice of sourdough, rye or home made bread*

*See page 6

Kenneth Keifer/ShutterStock

Zhekoss/ShutterStock

Beetroot and Chee

This is a stunningly robust salad, full of earthiness and sweetness. Any soft cheese will do – goat's cheese works well, but Hartington Dairy's Peakland White cheese is the perfect ingredient. If you choose to cook the beetroot from scratch, allow an hour in the oven, but vacuum-packed cooked beets do the job just as well.

Ingredients SERVES 4

6 medium sized cooked beetroots (room temperature)

250g crumbly cheese

For the dressing
2 tbsp white wine vinegar

½ tsp Dijon mustard

5 tbsp olive oil

1 tsp caraway seeds

Sea salt and freshly ground black pepper

Slices of home made bread* to serve   * See page 6

Method

1 Mix together the vinegar, mustard and seasoning. Beat the olive oil in with a whisk, bit by bit. Toast the caraway seeds lightly under the grill then add them to the dressing.

2 Cut the beets into thick slices, add the dressing, crumble the cheese into chunks and scatter through the beets. Serve with thick slices of home made bread.

Peakland White
(C) Hartington Cheese Company

noppharat/ShutterStock

Sweet Potato Bake

This 19th century recipe from Kedleston Hall in Derby (now owned by the National Trust) is suitable for vegetarians and makes good use of Sage Derby, a delicately nutty, semi-hard cheese marbled with sage, which has been made in Derbyshire for over 300 years.

Ingredients

500g sweet potatoes

25g ground cinnamon

115g crumbled Sage Derby

115g grated Farmhouse Cheddar

4 sage leaves

2 eggs

60ml milk

1 dessert spoon caster sugar

Method

1   Preheat the oven to 375F/190C/gas 5. Peel and dice the potatoes into large
    chunks and put in a pan with enough water to cover them. Bring to the boil
    and simmer for about 10 minutes, making sure they don't overcook.

2   Drain and place in a well-buttered ovenproof dish. Sprinkle with cinnamon,
    the sage leaves and then the cheeses. Beat the eggs, add the milk then pour
    over the potatoes and cheese.

3   Sprinkle the top with sugar and bake for about 25 minutes or until the top
    is golden brown. Served with green vegetables – green beans, broccoli or
    spring greens will do nicely.

mama_mia/ShutterStock

Hong Vo/ShutterStock

Seafood Chowde

This is a British take on a New England recipe. A satisfying, robust and nutritious fish soup, you can make it cheaply (leave out the prawns!) or push the boat out if you're feeling flush. Either way, it's absolutely delicious, easy to make – and very filling!

Ingredients

2 tbsp olive oil

2 rashers smoked bacon

1 clove garlic, finely chopped

1 red pepper, skin off* cut into fine strips

1 ltr stock (Marigold or a Kallo cube)

250g naturally smoked haddock

250g salmon

500g new potatoes

330g can of sweetcorn

Pinch of chilli flakes

A squeeze of tomato puree

Freshly ground black pepper

8 king prawns

Small carton single cream

Method

1   Gently heat the oil in a thick-bottomed casserole dish. Fry the bacon until it's starting to colour. Add the garlic, chilli flakes and red pepper followed by the stock, fish, sweet corn, potatoes and the tomato puree. Grind over some black pepper and simmer for about 20 minutes (or until the potatoes are cooked.)

2   Turn the heat right down and add the prawns and cream. Put the lid on the casserole and cook very gently for a further 10 minutes. Serve in big bowls with chunks of home made bread.

*to skin a pepper, cut it in half, take out the seeds and place under a hot grill until the skin chars. Then put into a plastic bag and leave for 10 minutes – the skin will come off in one fell swoop!

bitt24/ShutterStock

Fidgety Pie

This delicious savoury pie originates in South Derbyshire and was made for workers bringing in the harvest, ideal as it was portable and filling. Down the years it's been made with cider replacing the stock and gammon instead of bacon – it's been known for raisins to be added too. The name comes from the Anglo Saxon 'fitched' or 'five-sided', the shape the pie would originally have been. This recipe is similar to the one used by master baker Carol Cox in Tindalls, her fabulous bakery in Tideswell.

Ingredients MAKES 2 PIES

Pack of ready made short crust pastry or make your own - see page 14
. . . .
1 small onion, thinly sliced
. . . .
1 medium potato, thinly sliced
. . . .
1 apple, cored and finely sliced
. . . .
4 rashers of smoked bacon
. . . .
400ml beef stock
. . . .
Spring of thyme
. . . .
Sea salt
. . . .
Freshly ground black pepper
. . . .
1 medium egg, beaten, to glaze
. . . .

Method

1	Preheat the oven to 375C/190/gas 5
2	Fry the bacon until it's golden but not crispy. Layer the sliced potato, onion and apple in the bottom of each dish, sprinkling with seasoning and thyme. Add the bacon and finish with the remainder of the potato.
3	Pour over the beef stock (200ml per dish). Roll out the pastry on a lightly floured work surface then place on top of the dishes, crimping the edges. Make two slits in the top to allow steam to escape then brush with the beaten egg.
4	Bake for about 20 minutes until the pastry is golden.

Derbyshire Lobby

Lobby is a sort of hotpot – a dish made traditionally with salted or cured beef, onion and potato. Its origins are thought to be traced from North Staffordshire although it's commonplace throughout the country. In Derbyshire, it was eaten by working people, mainly farmers and potters who couldn't afford the more expensive cuts of meat. All sorts of ingredients would have been thrown in including pig's trotters and offal. This contemporary recipe still makes use of cheaper cuts of meat – add the trotters if you want to be old school! At home we'd have this on pancakes; Mum always made lots of batter and we had the meat on the first one, then ate the second sprinkled with sugar and half an orange squeezed over it.

Ingredients

450g stewing or braising steak, fat removed and cut into small chunks

Generous slug of vegetable oil

1 medium white onion, finely chopped

4 large potatoes, diced

1 swede, diced

4 celery sticks, chopped

4 carrots, chopped

Pearl barley

1 litre stock (see Basics or use Marigold Bouillon or Kallo stock cubes)

Sea salt

4 bay leaves

Freshly ground black pepper

Splash of malt vinegar (optional, but many Derbyshire cooks say this is an essential addition)

Basic pancake batter

115g plain or self raising flour
. . . .
Pinch of salt
. . . .
1 egg
. . . .
280ml milk
. . . .

Method

1   Heat the vegetable oil in a large pan. Add the onion and cook gently for 10 minutes until it's transparent but not browned. Add the carrot, celery and swede and cook for a further 10 minutes.

2   Remove the vegetables from the pan and put into a casserole pot – one with a lid. Heat another slug of oil in the pan and flash-fry the meat, sealing it. Add to the casserole along with the stock, barley, bay leaves and seasoning.

3   Cook in a medium hot oven for a couple of hours – the longer and slower you can cook it, the better.

4   For the pancakes, sift the flour and salt together. Add the lightly beaten egg. Add the milk gradually then beat with a whisk until you've got a creamy batter the consistency of single cream.

5   Heat a spoon of vegetable oil in a frying pan – when the fat's smoking hot, add a ladle of the batter. Turn the pancake after about 3 minutes and cook the other side – it should be starting to brown (I used to love the crispy bits round the edges!)

High Peak Lamb C

This traditional, wholesome, rustic stew is best made with lamb bred in a handful of farms in Derbyshire's glorious High Peak. Like most stews, this dish benefits from long cooking. Serve with floury or mashed potatoes, minted peas and a pile of pickled red cabbage (see Basics)

Ingredients

1 onion, finely sliced

1 clove garlic, crushed

1 large leek, chopped and washed

1 small turnip, diced

2 tsp rosemary, chopped

1 tsp parsley, chopped

1 tsp thyme, chopped

1 tsp oregano, chopped

Sea salt

Freshly ground black pepper

900g diced shoulder of lamb

1 litre stock (see Basics or use Marigold Bouillon or Kallo stock cubes)

28g pearl barley

28g plain flour, seasoned with salt & pepper

Oil for frying

For the dumplings

75g self raising flour

40g Atora suet

Sea salt

Freshly ground black pepper

1 tbsp chopped parsley

1 tbsp water

obbler

Method

1. In a large saucepan, warm some vegetable oil and add all the vegetables. Cook gently until they're transparent then add the herbs.

2. Whilst this is sweating, toss the diced lamb in the seasoned flour and fry briskly in batches in another pan, until it's browned. Add the vegetables to the meat, plus the pearl barley and mix thoroughly. Add the stock and seasoning. Stir well and cover.

3. Simmer for about 1 ½ hours, until the meat is tender.

For the dumplings

Put the flour, suet and parsley in a bowl. Season with salt & pepper. Stir in enough cold water to make a soft dough. Shape with floured hands into 8 balls. Uncover the casserole, pop the dumpling balls on top and leave the lid off. Cook for a further 20 minutes until the dumplings have risen.

Paul Cowan/ShutterStock

Derbyshire Sausage

Croots award winning farm shop in Duffield make and sell a wide variety of locally sourced meats and their fabulous tomato and basil sausages, made from mutton, lemon and herbs go beautifully in this easy, cheap and hearty dish – the kind of mid-week supper dish you can make the day before and warm up after a long day in the office.

Ingredients

6 Croots tomato & basil sausages

Carton of tomato passata

1 tin of red kidney beans

1 tin of butter beans

1 tsp English mustard

1 tbsp wholegrain mustard

1 tbsp harissa

4 tomatoes

Flat leaf parsley to garnish

Method

1   Preheat the oven to 450F/230C/gas 8. Grill the sausages for 10 minutes
    – don't let them brown, just cook through. Put the beans, passata, harissa
    and mustard into a casserole dish (one that has a lid). Cut the sausages into
    chunks, add them to the dish and stir everything thoroughly.

2   Cut the tomatoes in half and place on top. Cook for 30 minutes on the
    middle shelf. Sprinkle the parsley on top and serve piping hot with
    mashed potatoes.

apolonia/ShutterStock

Bakewell Pudding

The first thing to say is that there are puddings and tarts; Bakewell is famous for both but they're quite different. Legend has it that the pudding originated as a result of a mistake made by a cook at a local inn, but there's little proof of this. The earliest recipe given by Eliza Acton in 1845 is essentially an inch thick, rich custard of eggs yolks, butter, sugar and ratafia (almond essence) poured over a layer of jam and candied peel. Mrs Beeton had a recipe which omitted the peel and included ground almonds in the custard – a much nearer version of the one we enjoy today. The actual recipe is a trade secret, but this comes close.

Ingredients

500g ready made puff pastry

5tbsp seedless raspberry jam

100g unsalted butter

100g caster sugar

5 eggs

150g ground almonds

Almond essence

Method

1. Preheat the oven to 375F/190C/gas 5. Roll the pastry onto a lightly floured surface to form a circle a few inches larger than the tart tin. Carefully spread the jam evenly over the pastry base.

2. In a large mixing bowl, cream together the butter and sugar until pale and fluffy. Add the eggs one by one, beating well each time. Stir in equal amounts of the ground almonds after you've added the egg, stirring well until combined. Continue until all the eggs and ground almonds are used up then stir in the almond essence.

3. Pour the filling mixture into the pastry case and gently spread it evenly over the jam. Bake in the middle of the oven for 35-40 minutes until the surface is golden brown.

4. Dust with icing sugar once it's cooled and serve with a dollop of double cream.

Bakewell Pudding Shop

Ashbourne Ginge

Gingerbread men were made and sold in country towns at Easter Fairs and Autumn Wakes Weeks. Local legend has it the original recipe for this moreish biscuit came from French prisoners of war – in particular the personal chef of a captured French general who was detained in Ashbourne during the Napoleonic War. The delightful timber-framed Gingerbread Shop in the charming market town dates from the 15th century and makes a version very similar to this.

Ingredients

225g self raising flour
. . . .
2 tsp ground ginger
. . . .
1 tbsp golden syrup
. . . .
115g butter
. . . .
Pinch of salt
. . . .
115g soft brown sugar
. . . .

Magdalena Kucova/ShutterStock

Method

1. Preheat the oven to 350F/180C/gas 4. Sieve the flour, salt and ginger together. Cream the golden syrup, butter and sugar together then stir in the dry ingredients.

2. With your hands or a flat-bladed knife, knead the mixture on a floured surface until you've got a smooth dough. Roll out and cut into any shape you like – go mad with a cookie cutter!

3. Place on a greased baking sheet and bake in the oven for around 15 minutes – keep an eye on them or they'll burn!

Magdalena Kucova/ShutterStock

Buxton Pudding

This simple, tasty pudding was a great way of using up stale cake or bread and is still served in cafes in Buxton; in years gone by, farmer's wives would have taken it out into the fields for their hay-making husbands to eat by the slice! Serve piping hot with custard or cold – a slice goes beautifully with a cuppa. Make the pastry base by all means, but ready made will do nicely.

Ingredients

Packet of ready-made short-crust pastry*

For the filling

100g softened butter

100g caster sugar

2 medium eggs

150g plain cake crumbs (Madeira cake works well)

4 tbsp strawberry jam, gently warmed through

Method

1	Pre-heat the oven to 375F/190C/gas 5.
2	Roll the pastry out on a lightly floured work top to about 5mm thick. Line an 18cm flan dish with the pastry and spread the warmed jam over the base.
3	In a mixing bowl cream together the softened butter and caster sugar. Add the beaten eggs gradually then fold in the cake crumbs.
4	Put the mixture on top of the jam in the pastry case, spreading it out evenly. Sprinkle over a little caster sugar. Put the flan on a baking tray in the oven for about 25 minutes. When golden and baked through, remove. Eat it either hot with custard or cold with a cuppa.

*You could make your own pastry see page 14

Butter: Anna Sedneva/ShutterStock
Eggs: Imanhakim/ShutterStock
Sugar: nulinukas/ShutterStock

Ashover Moorland

An interesting combination of sweet and savoury ingredients, this delicious, filling pudding couldn't be easier to make and will become a firm family favourite. Like many sweet pies, it was fuel for farmers during harvest time all over Derbyshire.

Ingredients

Pack of short crust pastry

3 medium eggs, hard boiled

115g candied peel

115g currants

115g butter, warmed

170g sugar

Tart

Method

1   Preheat the oven to 350F/180C/gas 4. Roll the pastry out on a lightly floured work top. Line a flan dish with the pastry, pricking the bottom.

2   Mash the hard boiled eggs. Add all the other ingredients along with the warmed butter then put the mixture into the flan dish. Sprinkle a tbsp of sugar on the top and bake on the middle shelf of the oven until it's golden brown.

3   Serve with a dollop of crème fraiche or a scoop of ice cream.

Peel: nulinukas/ShutterStock
Sultanas: Svetlana Lukienko/ShutterStock
Butter: Anna Sedneva/ShutterStock

Bread and Butter P

A nursery tea time classic, this economical, delicious pudding will put a smile on every face round the table. A good pud will have a proper 'wobble'! Serve with crème fraiche or clotted cream.

Ingredients

8 slices of medium sliced white bread, crusts off

75g unsalted butter

60g sultanas

Grated zest of a lemon

220ml full fat milk

50g caster sugar

2 medium eggs

Vanilla essence

udding

Method

1 Preheat the oven at 190c/375F/gas 5. Butter the bread, cut into squares and put into a buttered dish, layering the bread with the sultanas and lemon zest. Beat the eggs with half the sugar and add the milk and vanilla essence.

2 Pour this custard over the bread mix and sprinkle the remaining sugar on the top, add a few sultanas to finish.

3 Cook on the middle shelf of the oven for 30 minutes, or until the top is golden brown.

4 Cool to just above room temperature before serving.

Jamie Rogers/ShutterStock

Derbyshire Rarebit

What makes this simple, delicious lunch or tea time favourite different from the classic Welsh rarebit is the addition of strong, nutty but sweet Hartington Dairy cheese and local craft beer.

Ingredients

4 slices thick bread, brown or white

2 tbsp plain flour

900g Hartington White Peakland cheese, crumbled

2 tsp English mustard powder

1 tsp cayenne pepper

400ml Buxton Brewery High Tor Red Ale (available in most supermarkets)

Generous splash Worcestershire Sauce

80g butter

Method

1   Gently melt the butter in a small, heavy-based saucepan. Gently whisk in the flour, mustard and cayenne pepper. Add the beer and relish, whisking all the time. Add the crumbled cheese, stirring until it's all melted.

2   Take off the heat and let it cool completely while you toast the bread. Pour the cheese mix over the toast then put under a hot grill until the whole thing is bubbling and golden.

Monkey Business Images/ShutterStock

Corned Beef Hash

An old family favourite, this hearty, easy to make comfort dish is a good way of using left over vegetables. A fried or poached egg turns this quick supper into a more substantial dinner.

Ingredients

400g swede, peeled and diced

700g potatoes, peeled and diced

300g carrots, peeled and diced

2 tbsp sunflower oil

1 red onion, peeled and thinly sliced

175g tin of corned beef

1 tbsp tomato puree

Dash of Worcestershire sauce

Freshly ground black pepper

Method

1   Bring a large pan of water to the boil and cook the diced swede for 5 minutes. Add the potatoes and carrots and cook for a further 10 minutes. Drain well.

2   Meanwhile, heat the oil in a large frying pan and add the onion. Cook over a medium heat until softened – be careful not to let them burn.

3   Roughly mash the drained vegetables so they still have some texture. Break the corned beef up and fold into the veg. Put it in the pan with the onions, add the tomato puree and Worcestershire sauce and mix well. Add a couple of twists of black pepper and continue cooking for a further 10 minutes, stirring gently until piping hot.

jabiru/Shutterstock

Toad in the Hole

This delicious dish would traditionally have had left over scraps from the Sunday roast in the hole; the humble sausage is a relatively recent idea. It's graced the dinner tables of Derbyshire farmers for centuries. The secret of beautifully risen batter is very hot fat; otherwise your puds will be a flop. Buy locally made sausages at the fabulous Chatsworth Farm Shop in Pilsley.

Ingredients

125g plain flour

½ tsp English mustard powder

2 eggs

300ml full fat milk

3 tbsp lard or dripping

Salt & black pepper

Dried thyme (optional)

6 pork sausages (or any of your choice)

Method

1   Set the oven at 220C/428F/gas 7. Whisk together the eggs and milk. Add
    a good pinch of salt and the thyme if using, then beat in the flour with the
    mustard powder.

2   Heat the lard or dripping in a small toasting tin or baking dish until it starts to
    smoke. Add the sausages and let them colour on all sides then pour in the
    batter. Bake for 25-30 minutes until risen and golden. Serve with piping hot
    onion gravy.

Monkey Business Images/ShutterStock

Butternut Squash &

This is a supremely warming, velvety winter soup, cheap and easy to make. Its dense, golden loveliness is enhanced with a swirl of cream on the top and if you're feeling flush, a scattering of croutons. The smell in the kitchen as this is cooking is worth the effort alone.

Ingredients

Splash of olive oil

1 large onion, finely chopped

1 butternut squash, peeled, de-seeded and chopped into chunks

1 red pepper, de-seeded and chopped into chunks

1 litre stock (see Basics or use Marigold Bouillon or Kallo cubes)

150ml skimmed milk

Sea salt

Freshly ground black pepper

Fresh chives or croutons, to garnish

Red Pepper Soup

Method

1. Warm the olive oil in a large pan and soften the onions. Add the squash, peppers and stock. Heat until simmering then cook gently for about 35 mins until the veg are tender.

2. Transfer to a blender and whizz until smooth. Return to the pan, add the milk and reheat. Season to taste.

3. Ladle into warm bowls. Swirl a dessert spoon of cream on the top of each one; add the chopped chives or croutons. This rewarding soup goes down well with a chunk of home made bread (see page 6).

Monkey Business Images/
ShutterStock

Macaroni Cheese

Hartington Bomber is a full fat, black waxed cheese made by the Hartington dairy from milk collected from local farms. Eat it on its own with crackers – it's a very satisfying lunch – but it cooks beautifully. This recipe calls for one or two more ingredients than a regular macaroni cheese but it's a winner, the family will love you for it. Serve with a simple green salad dressed with a squeeze of lemon – the richness of the dish needs a sharp accompaniment.

Ingredients SERVES 4

175g dry macaroni

1-2 tbsp olive oil

4 slices of smoked bacon cut into small pieces

1 medium onion, finely chopped

75g chestnut mushrooms, sliced

1 x 150g ball mozzarella cheese

300g tub of cheese sauce (most supermarkets do one)

2 tbsp crumbled Bomber cheese

1 bunch vine tomatoes

Sea salt

Freshly ground black pepper

Method

1   Preheat the oven to 375F/190C 190C/gas 5. Fill a large saucepan with water and bring it to the boil. Add a teaspoon of salt and a splash of olive oil. Add the macaroni and cook it for 5 minutes.

2   Meanwhile, heat the oil in a frying pan. Add the onion and bacon and cook for a couple of minutes, until both are golden brown. Add the mushrooms and cook for a further 2 minutes. Cut the mozzarella into smallish cubes.

3   Drain the pasta and put it into an oven-proof dish. Add the contents of the frying pan, the cheese sauce, the diced mozzarella and a good grinding of black pepper. Sprinkle the cheese over the top. Stir everything through and place the tomatoes (still on the vine) on top.

4   Drizzle olive oil on the tomatoes. Place the dish on the high shelf in your oven and bake for 20 minutes, or until the cheese is bubbling. Serve piping hot with a salad.

Elena Shashkina/ShutterStock

Spring Lamb Burg

Everyone has their favourite way of making burgers; after years of experimenting, lamb is my preferred choice of meat. Spring lamb is available to buy in many parts of Derbyshire, but JW Mettrick &Sons is a favourite butcher's shop in Glossop. I've added beaten egg and breadcrumbs at different times in an effort to bind the ingredients - in the end I've opted for the simple approach, which seems to work nicely. The ginger and cumin are optional but give the burger a piquant kick.

Ingredients

1 large onion, finely chopped

1kg roughly minced lamb

Knob of fresh ginger, grated

1 tsp ground cumin

1/2 tsp chilli flakes

2 tsp chopped herbs (rosemary or thyme work well)

Sea salt

Freshly ground black pepper

Garnishes, sauces and rolls, as desired

Method

1   In a large bowl combine all the ingredients thoroughly with your hands (top tip, wet your hands to stop the meat from sticking). Divide the meat into 12 flattish burgers. Cover and refrigerate for an hour. In the meantime, spark up your barbeque.

2   Cook the burgers on a medium to hot barbecue or griddle pan: leave them undisturbed for the first 3 minutes so they build up a good seal on the bottom, then carefully turn them over, adding a slice of cheese on top if desired. Cook for a further 4 minutes for rare, and 7 for well done, and allow to rest for a few minutes before serving. (You can toast buns, cut-side down, on the barbecue at this point.)

Expoz Photography/ShutterStock

Cottage Pie

Cottage pie (made with beef) or Shepherd's pie (made with lamb) are the kings of comfort food, can be made a day in advance (tastes even better) and represents great value for money! Franjoy Dairy in Hazelwood, near Belper makes a fabulous hard, nutty cheese, a handful of which sprinkled on top of your pie finishes it off beautifully.

Ingredients SERVES 4

Vegetable oil

100g lean beef mince

1 large onion, finely chopped

1 carrot, finely chopped

2 celery sticks, finely chopped

Clove garlic, finely chopped

6 mushrooms, sliced

1 sprig thyme

200ml stock (See Basics, or use Marigold Bouillon)

Worcester Sauce

1 tin chopped tomatoes

450g potatoes

Knob of butter

Salt

Freshly ground black pepper

Handful of grated cheese

Method

1	Heat a tablespoon of oil in a large pan and gently brown the mince. Remove and add the chopped vegetables to the pan. Cook for about five minutes or until they've softened a bit.
2	Add the mince, a good dash of relish, the tomatoes, stock, thyme and season generously with salt & pepper. Let it bubble away for about an hour, until the stock has reduced by half.
3	In the meantime, peel the potatoes, cut them into small-ish chunks, put in cold water with a pinch of salt and bring to the boil. Let them simmer away for about 20 minutes, until they're soft.
4	Drain, add a knob of butter, a splash of milk, and mash. Put the mince mixture into an ovenproof dish, cover with the mashed potatoes, sprinkled on the cheese and put in a medium hot oven for about 15 minutes until the cheese has browned up. Serve with minted peas and pickled red cabbage*

*See page 12

violeta pasat/ShutterStock

Store Cupboard Staples

Atora suet	Honey
Bay leaves	Instant yeast sachets
Black peppercorns	Jar of pitted black olives
Block of parmesan	Kallo stock cubes
Candied peel	Lime juice
Caster sugar	Marigold Swiss Vegetable Bouillon
Chilli flakes	Olive oil
Cider vinegar	Pearl barley
Dijon mustard	Plain white flour
Dried macaroni	Raisins
Dried oregano	Raspberry jam
Dried pasta	Ready made filo pastry
Dried sage leaves	Ready made short crust pastry
Dried thyme	Red wine vinegar
English mustard	Sea salt (Maldon is the best, but any will do)
Fine oatmeal	Strong white bread flour
Fresh ginger	Sunflower oil
Golden syrup	Tinned butter beans
Ground almonds	Tinned chopped tomatoes
Ground cinnamon	Tinned red kidney beans
Ground coriander	White wine vinegar
Ground cumin	Whole nutmeg
Harissa	Worcester sauce

About
Amanda **Wragg**

Amanda Wragg is a freelance food and feature writer, born in Derbyshire and now based near Hebden Bridge on the Pennines. She writes for the Yorkshire Post, Alastair Sawday, Square Meal and the AA. She sits on several judging panels for regional and national food & drink awards, inspects and writes for a well-known restaurant review publication and co-writes a website dedicated to good places to eat and stay in Yorkshire, **www.squidbeak.co.uk**

About
Joan **Ransley**

Joan Ransley is a food photojournalist based in Ilkley, West Yorkshire. She works for local and national publications including The Yorkshire Post, Yorkshire Life, Derbyshire Life, The University of Leeds, The Guardian and the online Travel Magazine – Food Tripper. Joan is a member of the Guild of Food Writers. **www.joanransley.co.uk**